EXPLORE THE UNITED STATES

NEW HAMPSHIRE

Julie Murray

Big Buddy Books

An Imprint of Abdo Publishing
abdobooks.com

abdobooks.com

Published by Abdo Publishing, a division of ABDO, PO Box 398166, Minneapolis, Minnesota 55439. Copyright © 2020 by Abdo Consulting Group, Inc. International copyrights reserved in all countries. No part of this book may be reproduced in any form without written permission from the publisher. Big Buddy Books™ is a trademark and logo of Abdo Publishing.

Printed in the United States of America, North Mankato, Minnesota
102019
012020

THIS BOOK CONTAINS
RECYCLED MATERIALS

Design: Aruna Rangarajan, Mighty Media, Inc.
Production: Mighty Media, Inc.
Editor: Liz Salzmann

Cover Photograph: Shutterstock Images
Interior Photographs: aleroy4/iStockphoto, p. 30 (top); BirdImages/iStockphoto, p. 30 (bottom); DenisTangneyJr/iStockphoto, pp. 9 (bottom right), 10, 11, 14, 15; EJJohnsonPhotography/iStockphoto, p. 24 (inset); Jeffrey Joseph/Wikimedia Commons, p. 27; Jim Cole/AP Images, p. 29 (middle); lennjo/iStockphoto, pp. 4, 5; Library of Congress, pp. 21, 26 (bottom right); NASA/Wikimedia Commons, pp. 22, 23, 27 (left); Shutterstock Images, pp. 4 (state seal), 6, 7, 9, 11 (inset), 13, 16, 17, 18, 19, 24, 25, 26, 28, 29, 30; US Senate Photo Studio/Frank A F/Wikimedia Commons, p. 20; Woodkern/iStockphoto, pp. 9 (top right), 26 (bottom left)

Populations figures from census.gov

Library of Congress Control Number: 2019943166

Publisher's Cataloging-in-Publication Data
Names: Murray, Julie, author.
Title: New Hampshire / by Julie Murray
Description: Minneapolis, Minnesota : Abdo Publishing, 2020 | Series: Explore the United States | Includes online resources and index.
Identifiers: ISBN 9781532191329 (lib. bdg.) | ISBN 9781532178054 (ebook)
Subjects: LCSH: U.S. states--Juvenile literature. | Northeastern States--Juvenile literature. | Physical geography--United States--Juvenile literature. | New Hampshire--History--Juvenile literature.
Classification: DDC 974.2--dc23

CONTENTS

CHAPTER 1

ONE NATION

The United States is a diverse country. It has farmland, cities, coasts, and mountains. Its people come from many different backgrounds. And, its history covers more than 200 years.

Today the country includes 50 states. New Hampshire is one of these states. Let's learn more about this state and its story!

DID YOU KNOW?

New Hampshire became a state on June 21, 1788. It was the ninth state to join the nation.

The White Mountain National Forest covers 10 percent of New Hampshire.

CHAPTER 2

NEW HAMPSHIRE UP CLOSE

The United States has four main regions. New Hampshire is in the Northeast.

New Hampshire has three states on its borders. Massachusetts is south. Vermont is west, and Maine is east. The country of Canada is north. And, the Atlantic Ocean is southeast.

New Hampshire is a small state. Its total area is 9,349 square miles (24,214 sq km). About 1.3 million people live there.

DID YOU KNOW?
Washington, DC, is the US capital city. Puerto Rico is a US commonwealth. This means it is governed by its own people.

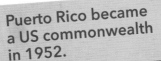

Puerto Rico became a US commonwealth in 1952.

Regions of the United States

West
Midwest
South
Northeast

CANADA

WASHINGTON
MONTANA
NORTH DAKOTA
SOUTH DAKOTA
MINNESOTA
MICHIGAN
NEW HAMPSHIRE
VERMONT
MAINE
OREGON
IDAHO
WYOMING
WISCONSIN
PENNSYLVANIA
MASSACHUSETTS
CALIFORNIA
NEVADA
UTAH
COLORADO
NEBRASKA
IOWA
ILLINOIS
INDIANA
OHIO
NEW YORK
RHODE ISLAND
CONNECTICUT
NEW JERSEY
ARIZONA
NEW MEXICO
KANSAS
MISSOURI
KENTUCKY
DELAWARE
MARYLAND
WASHINGTON, DC
WEST VIRGINIA
VIRGINIA
OKLAHOMA
ARKANSAS
TENNESSEE
NORTH CAROLINA
SOUTH CAROLINA
TEXAS
ALABAMA
GEORGIA
FLORIDA
MISSISSIPPI
LOUISIANA

PACIFIC OCEAN

MEXICO

Gulf of Mexico

ATLANTIC OCEAN

ALASKA

HAWAII

PUERTO RICO

N
W E
S

7

CHAPTER 3

IMPORTANT CITIES

Concord is New Hampshire's capital. It is also the state's third-largest city, with 43,412 people. This city's history dates to the 1720s. It has a historic downtown and Main Street.

Manchester is the largest city in the state. It is home to 112,525 people. It is known for its strong business community.

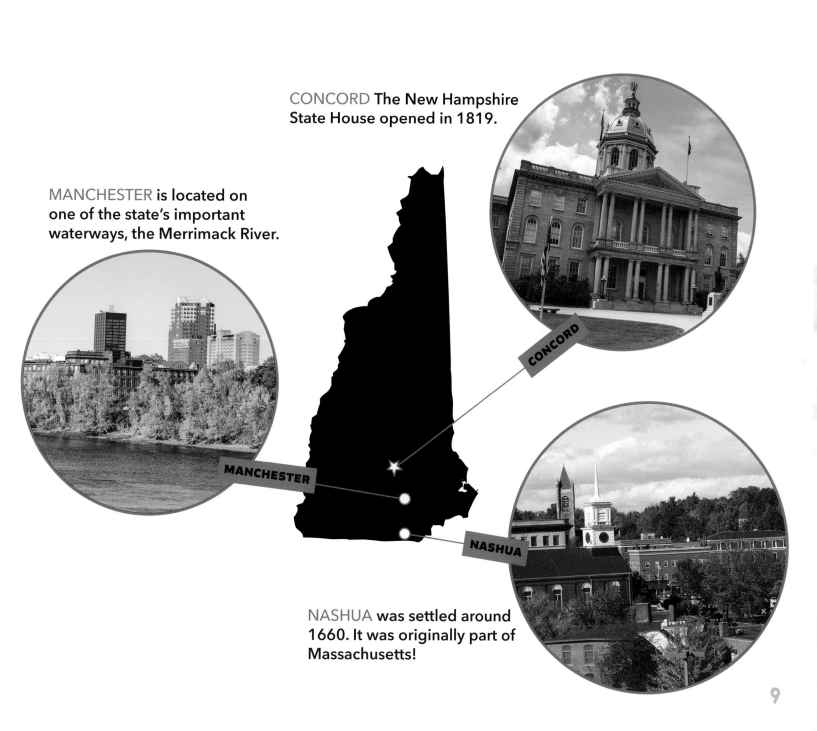

CONCORD The New Hampshire State House opened in 1819.

MANCHESTER is located on one of the state's important waterways, the Merrimack River.

CONCORD

MANCHESTER

NASHUA

NASHUA was settled around 1660. It was originally part of Massachusetts!

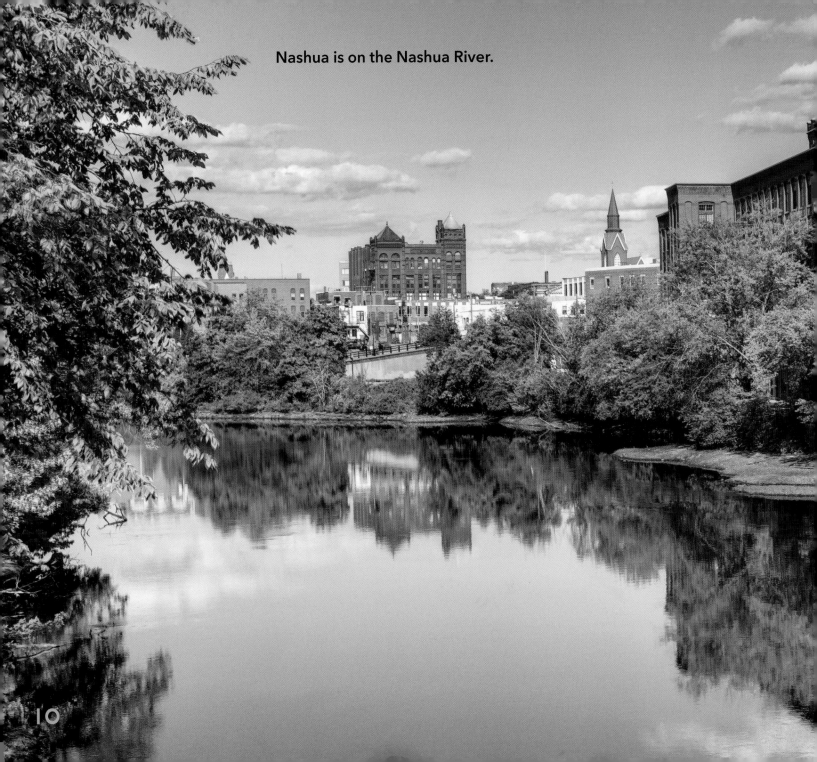

Nashua is on the Nashua River.

Nashua (NA-shuh-wuh) is New Hampshire's second-largest city. It is home to 89,246 people. This city is close to the state of Massachusetts. It is near Silver Lake State Park. People swim and picnic there.

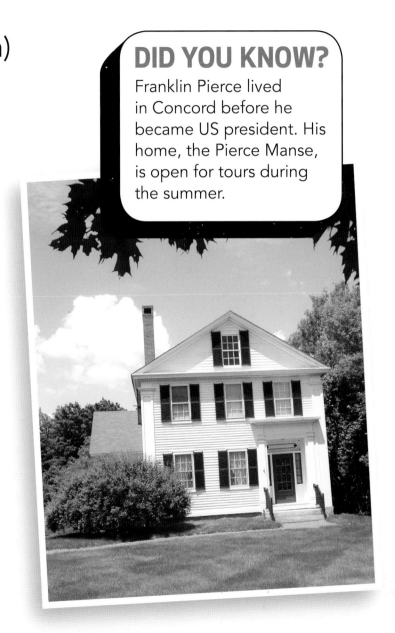

CHAPTER 4

NEW HAMPSHIRE IN HISTORY

New Hampshire's history includes settlers and war. New Hampshire began as an English colony in the 1600s. The first settlers arrived in 1623.

In the 1700s, colonists wanted to be part of a new country. So, they fought in the Revolutionary War and formed the United States. In 1788, New Hampshire became the ninth state.

DID YOU KNOW?
Native Americans lived in present-day New Hampshire for thousands of years before the colony formed.

Captain John Smith of England was one of the first Europeans to visit New Hampshire. He came to the area around 1614.

CHAPTER 5

ACROSS THE LAND

New Hampshire has hills, forests, lakes, and rivers. The White Mountains cover part of the state. The Connecticut and Merrimack Rivers flow through New Hampshire. Also, part of the state borders the Atlantic Ocean.

Many types of animals make their homes in New Hampshire. These include moose, white-tailed deer, and beavers.

DID YOU KNOW?

In July, the average high temperature in New Hampshire is 79.5°F (26.4°C). In January, it is 28.5°F (-1.9°C).

Lake Winnipesaukee is the largest lake in the state.

CHAPTER 6

EARNING A LIVING

New Hampshire has many important businesses. Some people have jobs helping visitors to the state. Others work in manufacturing jobs making electronics and paper. People in the state also work in finance, education, and health care.

New Hampshire has many natural resources. Mines produce sand, gravel, and granite. Farms provide apples, dairy products, cattle, and hay.

Lobsters and fish are caught off of New Hampshire's coast.

CHAPTER 7

NATURAL WONDER

The White Mountains are in northern New Hampshire. Their most famous area is called the Presidential Range. Eight of its peaks are named after US presidents.

Mount Washington is the most famous mountain peak in the range. It is known for having wild weather. In April 1934, the wind speed there was recorded at 231 miles per hour (372 kmh). That was the world record until 1996.

Mount Washington is the highest point in New Hampshire. It stands 6,288 feet (1,917 m) tall!

CHAPTER 8

HOMETOWN HEROES

Many famous people are from New Hampshire. Franklin Pierce was born in Hillsborough in 1804. He was the fourteenth US president. Pierce served from 1853 to 1857. During this time, the country faced disagreements that led to the American Civil War.

DID YOU KNOW?

Jeanne Shaheen became the first female governor of New Hampshire in 1997. In 2008, she was the first woman from New Hampshire to be elected to the US Senate.

Pierce is the only
US president from
New Hampshire.

Astronaut Alan B. Shepard Jr. was born in East Derry in 1923. On May 5, 1961, he became the first American to travel in space.

Christa McAuliffe was born in 1948 in Boston, Massachusetts. She later worked as a teacher in Concord. McAuliffe was chosen as the first teacher and non-astronaut to go into space. In 1986, she boarded the space shuttle *Challenger*. Sadly, it exploded after liftoff. McAuliffe and the other astronauts died.

McAuliffe had planned to teach lessons from space.

Shepard's first spaceflight was part of Project Mercury. His space capsule was called the *Freedom 7*.

CHAPTER 9

A GREAT STATE

The story of New Hampshire is important to the United States. The people and places that make up this state offer something special to the country. Together with all the states, New Hampshire helps make the United States great.

Umbagog Lake is on the border between New Hampshire and Maine.

New Hampshire has only
18 miles (29 km) of coastline.
Much of it is rugged and rocky.

TIMELINE

1788

New Hampshire became the ninth state on June 21.

1833

The Peterborough Public Library was established. It was one of the first in the United States.

1861

The **American Civil War** began. New Hampshire fought for the Northern states.

1700s

1800s

Concord became New Hampshire's **capital**.

1808

Franklin Pierce of Hillsborough became the fourteenth US president.

1853

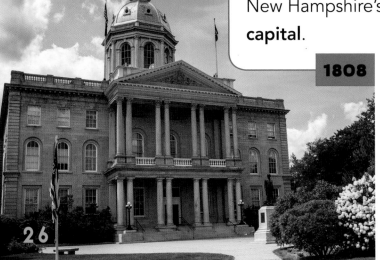

26

2003

The Old Man of the Mountain broke off and fell to the ground. This rock formation was one of the state's famous landmarks.

1961

Alan B. Shepard Jr. of East Derry became the first American in space.

1900s

New Hampshire hosted the Bretton Woods Conference. The World Bank was founded at this important event.

1944

Jeanne Shaheen became New Hampshire's first female governor.

1997

2000s

New Hampshire held the nation's first US presidential **primary** of the year on February 11. This is one of the first major voting steps in choosing a president.

2020

27

TOUR BOOK

Do you want to go to New Hampshire? If you visit the state, here are some places to go and things to do!

DISCOVER

Walk the grounds of Dartmouth College in Hanover. This well-known school was founded in 1769.

REMEMBER

Check out the Gorham Historical Society & Railroad Museum. It is located in an old train station.

You can see steam engines and other historical exhibits.

PLAY

Ski in New Hampshire's mountains in the winter.

In the summer, you can ride a ski lift for a great view!

SEE

Spend the day at the McAuliffe-Shepard Discovery Center in Concord. There, you can visit a planetarium and learn about space travel.

EXPLORE

Visit the White Mountain National Forest. Many people like to hike its trails.

FAST FACTS

▶ **STATE FLOWER**
Purple Lilac

▶ **STATE TREE**
White Birch

▶ **STATE BIRD**
Purple Finch

▶ STATE FLAG:

▶ NICKNAME:
Granite State

▶ DATE OF STATEHOOD:
June 21, 1788

▶ POPULATION (RANK):
1,356,458
(41st most-populated state)

▶ TOTAL AREA (RANK):
9,349 square miles
(46th largest state)

▶ STATE CAPITAL:
Concord

▶ POSTAL ABBREVIATION:
NH

▶ MOTTO:
"Live Free or Die"

GLOSSARY

American Civil War—the war between the Northern and Southern states from 1861 to 1865.

astronaut—a person who is trained for space travel.

capital—a city where government leaders meet.

diverse—made up of things that are different from each other.

granite—a type of very hard rock often used for building.

primary—an election before the main election in which members of the same political party run against each other. Voters choose candidates to run in the main election.

region—a large part of a country that is different from other parts.

resource—a supply of something useful or valued.

Revolutionary War—a war fought between England and the North American colonies from 1775 to 1783.

ONLINE RESOURCES

Booklinks
NONFICTION NETWORK
FREE! ONLINE NONFICTION RESOURCES

To learn more about New Hampshire, please visit **abdobooklinks.com** or scan this QR code. These links are routinely monitored and updated to provide the most current information available.

INDEX